MADNESS
AND A BIT OF
HOPE

MADNESS AND A BIT OF HOPE

POEMS BY SAFIYA HENDERSON-HOLMES

HARLEM RIVER PRESS
New York City

Published for **HARLEM RIVER PRESS** by:
WRITERS AND READERS PUBLISHING, INC.
P.O. BOX 461, Village Station,
New York, New York 10014

Cover Design: Janice Walker
Book Design: Tenth Avenue Editions, Inc.

ISBN 0-86316-135-9 Hardcover
ISBN 0-86316-136-7 Paperback
0 9 8 7 6 5 4 3 2 1

Manufactured in the United States of America

madness
dedicated to
naimah lateefah holmes,
my daughter, friend
and spirit

.

.

and thanking marie brown, endlessly, endlessly

.

.

contents

·

·

madness

madness

.
.

casualties

.

.

the consumers are dying
they cannot afford

to bury themselves
fully dressed

they stand on sidewalks
everywhere

as if by the will
of a traffic light

they await
the fall

homelessness

.

.

without a garden
or a pot to piss in

all nine lives in debt
this one repeating itself

like a damaged record
dull needle still cutting deeply

music sucks in the panhandle
too crowded to dance to a damn thing

inner city housing

.

.

gimme a condo
800,000 dollars in the air

gimme overpasses
tunnels to every train

and store
and let's swear

by our white collars
that i won't see

those beggars
beggin change from me

who gives a good flying fuck
.

.

who falls in love
these days, everybody hovers

too many damn tests
the negative showing positive

is still negative
too many graves to walk over

love at first sight
dead on a hummer

a rubber ain't a rose
but, who gives a good flying fuck

wounds #1

.

.

into the hour of
the purple sky the parents

fought nightly, then slept
under a heavy cover

of war, in the meek
quiet of the bedroom door

their two children stood guard
three foot sentries staring them

selves to death, as the
blood rose slowly on the walls

wounds #13

.

.

she was there, on her
hands and knees when the

baby came, feet first
with eyes of an owl

and the fist her husband
hit her with

birthmarking its skin
no one cried

afferent #3
(creature comforts)

.

.

all it takes
still

is one thin
sharp blade

a hairline
two inches

across
a short trip

five blades
for a dollar

metropolis nyc, 42nd st, 8th ave, 1989

.

.

within the hardened cement
shiny bits of mica

dazzling the eye
above the cement

hardened people beg
for bits

shine and dazzle
long removed

wounds #6

.

.

underground too long
on a new york city subway

crowded inside, a man
with a gun shoots

four other men out
of his way, he breathes

deeper in the ever
enlarging space

afferent #1
(a riddle of sorts)

.

.

when making love
in new york city

i break for sirens
and have a ten second

hold for gun shots
what am i

lunatics on parade
(or the death of yusef hawkins, age 16, a black
youth attacked and killed in bensonhurst brooklyn
new york, 8/23/89)

.

.

the music screams from somewhere
an old, tired tune

even the costumes are familiar
the spit, the cutting stares

the bullet words fired
at anyone or anything unwanted

but the players are younger
accepting their position

from the elders, the hoods
are more fashionable

proudly showing faces
the band leader raises a fist, or a bat

or a gun, the highstepping begins
the first back is broken

one too different to remain whole
the sound of bat against bone

will continue into night
no one will sleep

blood passes around
like cold beer

homelessness #2
(33rd st., 7th ave, nyc, 1989)

.

.

the avenue is crowded
with the possibility
of uselessness

parts of whole families
gather by corner curbs
and count the number

of yellow cars going by
taxis not included
competition is fierce

a massive hunt for yellow
in the evening scores will be added
winners will take all they can get

.

failure of an invention

.

.

i am not any of the faces
you have put on me america

every mask has slipped
i am not any of the names

or sounds you have called me
the tones have nearly

made me deaf
this dark skin, both of us

have tried to bleach
i can smell the cancer.

this thick hair, these thick lips
both of us have tried to narrow

begging entrance through
the needle of your eye

some of me broken
in the squeeze

and even as I carry
a bone of yours in my back

your soul america
no matter what we've tried

i've never been able to bear

the battle, over and over again
(given as testimony in support of the student's case
against racism at columbia university)

·

·

my daughter came home from school one day
when she was four
she ran into the bathroom, crying and
sitting on the floor

i said, —baby, what's the matter, c'mon,
what could be so bad
i bought you a box of cherry fun fruits,
bet that'll make you glad —

she lifted up her little arms, squinted in the light
mommy, she asked, —why didn't god make me white —

she dropped her arms and question hard on her lap
her eyes were closed, my knees were weak, she said,

—they keep saying i'm ugly, and they say
it's because i'm black —
the bathroom had always been our place we ran to
whenever she was hurt

we'd bandaide the cuts, pull out the splinters
and wash away the dirt
but suddenly our refuge had become a place for war

with bombs waiting to explode
the sink's faucet dripped like a timer,
the pipes signaled an enemy code

who said these things, i wanted to ask,
but i didn't let out the words
my child picking away her dark brown skin
had loosened every nerve

and who was not important, more important was the why
that in 1983 america, racism, was making my child cry

i sat beside her on the floor, pulled her to my chest
i thought of how often we had sat like this
just to take a rest

—sweetheart —i said, —now you know you're not ugly —
i pasted words in the air,

—you're one of the prettiest girls i've ever seen, anywhere —
her back was warm and sweaty, she held her muscles tight

there was sand on her cheeks,
she was much too young to fight
the air was full of bullet holes, i could smell the dead

—and you have the prettiest smile —
my daughter shook her head
i pushed against that bathroom wall,
trying to gain a balance

trying to find the perfect words
to break this painful silence
i thought of all the great ones
who had died to prevent such a day

the fannie lous, malcolms,
name calling dragons that they slayed
i thought about the marches,
shouts of let freedom ring

busrides, boycotts, sit-ins, speeches, endless praying
the world stood boldly in my bathroom,
between my child and me

and i wondered as i squeezed her hands,
how long will the battle be
her eyes opened and looked in mine,
as if she heard my fear

she hugged my neck and said, —mommy, i don't care,
they're two mean boys and they're always starting fights

they never have anything special for lunch,
they always ask for bites —
she straightened and coughed,
her arms still around my neck

— and i'm going to take my fun fruits to school,
and they won't get a peck —
she said, — and the bigger one is going to ask
until his face gets red —

she wiped her eyes, rubbed sand from her head
pointed to her left arm, swallowed and said,

— one thing i know, —
she placed her hands on her hips,
i saw her strength begin to grow,

— mommy, his face gets like that when he's mad,
i seen it lots of times
mommy, i think his face is more ugly than mine —

i kissed her softly on her mouth, both her sandy cheeks
washed her face, and studied the draining water
as if it were the last enemy's retreat

rape, a class act

.

.

if she's born
and educated ivy league

and if the ivy
grows in her hair

without any of
her roots showing

and if her hair
blows in the wind

and if the wind
resonates like a cash register

and if the cash register
is full, fuller than her breast

or her lips
and some individual

rapes her
getting involved in her ivy

and her cash flow
busting up her register

then, by all means
we have a case on our hands

a crime, an old fashioned
news story to sink teeth into

otherwise, folks
it's a mere screw, bound to happen

for tawana brawley
(for us)

.

.

women, calling all the women
the mothers, daughters, sisters,
granmas, aunties, girlfriends,
high flying, high stepping, far reaching
career ladies, sweet sweet
girls with the claws between their legs, dandelion

daydreaming girls
women, calling all of us here, all of us now
we black, we red, we white, we yellow, we deaf, we mute,
we see too much women
come here to this spot in our heart, in our gut

where the blood and nerve are thickest and most wicked
to that center, that cyst, that tumor,
that nipple where it begins
and ends drastically and always
calling every single one of us titties

us hips, us umbilicals, us clits
every single one of us madams, missies,
mrs. cuties, dearies
to this jack hammer spot,
this nasty mass of promises spot

this crude oil spot, this blessing spot, this baptismal spot
come here, right now, hurry 'cause
somebody took one of our babies,
somebody took one of our she / girl
one of our she / precious, she / so young / and has such a
long way to go girls
somebody jumped into her everything and everywhere
her dreamtime and woman magic
somebody defecated in the eye of her forever

somebody stuffed her just getting there body
into an ungodly, unearthly, inhuman,
pissed stained plastic bag
and left her to simmer in the woods
of somebody's nightmare
somebody ran over her she / wasn't even thinking of such

breast
all over her baby doll belly
all over her junior highschool walk
somebody ripped open her springtime
killing her roses, her daisies, her violets, her lilies

somebody jammed her star memories,
her karma songs, her universal prayers,
women, calling all us women
us she / power, us moon witches,
us venus hawks, us christ bearers
come here, right here to this blood rock,
this love lump, this wish callous, and hurry,
bring your eternities, every ounce of your infinity
hurry, right now and forever, that she / child needs us,
every piece of us,
she / child needs us now

coming to term
(written on the 17th anniversary of roe vs. wade)

·

·

1.
it is more than birds and bees
and being born
beyond the womb
it is how many women on their hands and knees
scrubbing how many floors, ammonia eating
which parts of their skin, clouding which eye
love in the weight of how many children

2.
it is how many men burning
how many hours from their brain for how much pay
into how much beer, trying to become sons again,
anyone's son
passing the buck and the ball

3.
it is how many mouths know the shape
and size of hunger
which pieces getting caught in whose throat
at what age can someone suck hunger dry
handle it as sand, erecting castles stiffened with phlegm

4.
beyond the womb
further and further beyond the womb
it is how many houses are being built
how many schools, how many hospitals, how many parks,
how many buses,
how many trains, and where

5.
between whose legs
at the count of whose breath
in the push of whose ability
in the opening of whose eye
in the cry of whose history
in the arms of whose concern
in the naming of whose worth

6.
beyond the womb
swollen breast have been raped
because of their smell
swollen breast have been shot
because of their color
swollen breast have been flung into fire
because of their preferences

7.
beyond the womb
pulsing like fist
umbilicals have been used to hang men
umbilicals have been used to whip women
umbilicals have been used to maim children

8.
beyond the womb
arms and legs are paralyzed by touch
beyond the womb
layers of flesh come to term
in a skeleton's lap

9.
beyond the womb
layers of flesh
come to term in a skeleton's lap
count the days
count the days

rituals of spring
(for the 78th anniversary of the shirtwaistfactory fire)

.

.

from bareness to fullness flowers do bloom
whenever, however spring enters a room
oh, whenever, however spring enters a room

march 25th, 1911
at the triangle shirtwaist factory
a fire claimed the lives of 146 people, mostly women,
mostly children in the plume of their lives,
in the room of their lives
begging for spring, toiling and begging for spring

and in my head
as i read the history, afraid to touch the pictures
i imagine the room, i imagine the women
dressed in pale blues and pinks,
some without heads or arms — sitting
some without legs or waist — hovering
hundreds of flowering girls tucking spring into sleeves,
tucking and tugging at spring to stay alive

and so a shirtwaist for spring
a dress with a manish collar, blousing over breast,
blousing over sweat, tapering to fit a female waist,
tapering to fit a female breath
sheer silk, cotton, linen
hand done pleats, hands done in by pleats
hands done in by darts and lace

colors of spring
pale blues, pale pinks, yellows, magentas, lavender, peach,

secret thoughts of spring
falling in love under a full moon, forever young
with money enough to buy a flower or two,
time enough to smell it
yes, from bareness to fullness a flower will bloom
anytime, everytime spring enters a room
and here, near these machines, hundreds of flowering
girls

shirtwaist factory room 1911
crowded, hard, fast, too fast, closed windows,
locked doors, smell of piss, of sweat,
of wishes being cut to bits,
needle stabs, electric shocks, miscarriages over silk,
fading paisley, fading magenta,
falling in love will get you fired, forever old,
never fast enough, buying flowers is wasteful
so hurry, hurry, grind your teeth and soul
six dollars a week send to grandfather,
four dollars a week send to aunt ruth, sleep over the
machine and you're done for, way before you open your
eyes ma'm, madam, miss, mrs. mother, girlie
hundreds of flowering green spring girls in rows
waiting with needles in hands for spring to show

women workers
from ireland, poland, germany, france,
england, grenada, mississippi
thin clothes, thinner hopes, months full of why,
of how, of when
answers always less than their pay
but the sewing machines grew like weeds,
thick snake roots strangling the flowers everyday
strangling the roses, daises, lilies everyday
hundreds of blooming girls
hundreds of blooming, spring girls

the shirtwaist building 1911
135 feet high, wooden, cold, three floors,
not enough stairs,
one fire escape ending in mid-air,
ending in the spring mid-air
a tender room of hundreds of blooming bright girls
hundreds of daisy bud girls who pray for spring
to enter their world,
who pray and sweat for spring to enter their world

the strike the year before
and they shouted; open the doors,
unwire the windows, more air,
more stairs, more quiet time, more fire escapes
and to the ground damn you,
and more toilets, more time to be sick,
more time to be well,
and remove the fear and slow it down,
for god's sake, slow it all time, it's spring

they shouted
hundreds of flowering girls,
hundreds of flowering girls shouted
for spring to hurry, hurry and enter their world

and
triangle won a half day
but the doors remained locked,
windows remained wired, no extra air,
no extra quiet time, or sick time, the fear stayed,
nothing slowed
and god watched hundreds of flowering girls twirl
hundreds of flowering girls willow and twirl

march 25th 1911 at triangle
a worker is expendable

a sewing needle is not

a worker is bendable
a sewing needle is not
a worker can be sent straight to hell
a sewing needle is heaven sent
and must be protected well
a sewing needle is the finger of god
and must be protected well
over hundreds of flowering girls,
hundreds of flowering sweet dandelion girls

march 25th, smoke
smoke, stopping the machines
run to wired windows, run to locked doors,
run to the one and only fire escape,
everyone run to the air
hundreds of flowering girls

smoke
stopping eyes, stopping hearts, stopping worlds
elevator move faster, elevator you are a machine
managed by a human being move faster, c'mon faster
carry all the flowering girls, carry all the sweet,
sweet orchid girls

fire
catching bouquets of girls in a corner, tall, long
stemmed lilies on fire in a corner,
from bloom to ashes in a corner, smell
them in the rain hundreds of tulip girls

on a window ledge
pelees for life, on a window ledge lovely, ribboned young
ladies on their tiptoes twirling, twirling
an arabesque for life
hundreds of flowering girls
smell them in the rain
hundreds of jasmine girls

the ladders were too short
the hoses were too short
the men holding the nets were not gods, only men
who were never trained to catch falling bodies, or
falling stars, or hundreds of flowering girls, hundreds
of carnation bud girls

and the girls
were girls not angels jumping,
not goddesses flying or hovering
they smashed, they broke into
large pieces, smell them in the rain

and the sidewalks
opened in shame to meet the flowering girls
the sidewalks opened in such horrible shame to cradle
the remains of violets
and the gutters
bled for hours, choking on bones, shoes, buttons,
ribbons, holy sewing needles
the gutters bled for hours all the colors of spring
the cool magenta of delicate spring

and the fire ate
the locked doors and the wired windows,
ate the fast machines
in their narrow rooms, ate the lace and hand done pleats,
the silk, the cotton, the linen,

the crisp six dollars a week, the
eternal buzz of someone else's dreams
nightmares and screams of quiet girls,
loud skull cracking noises from shy girls
smell them in the rain, the lilacs, daffodils
in the rain

spring, 78 years later
triangle is now part of a university, with offices
and polished intellect, arched unwired windows,
hydraulically controlled and unlocked doors,
air conditioning, swivel chairs, marble walls and fire
alarms

but oh, hundreds of flowering girls still roam
hundreds of blushing spring girls still roam
78 years later in the paint, in the chrome
in the swivel of the chairs
hundreds of blossoms twirling in the air
daring to descend if ever, oh ever the fire comes again

yes, like lead they will drop
if ever, oh ever the fire comes again
to hundreds of flowering girls
smell them in the rain, iris, peonies, magnolias,
bending for the rain

peace yall
(or do the do / wop / drop)

.

.

people on line two blocks deep
for government butter, government cheese,
government, government please

is this a break, will it lower unemployment,
lessen the power of the state
look closely, more than bees in the honey

more than flies in the state butter
space shuttle cutters
and cheese lines won't end depression

cheese lines won't end u.s. intervention
doesn't cover up the government's intention
of finding new ways to make people submit

finding new and cheaper ways to make people
sit and watch gong shows
where no one has a winning act

no houses being pulled from hats
no pennies changing into twenties
no whites turning black

yo, big mac
if jr wants to leave the show
he can push a button and everyone goes

we're talking sudden here, swift
boom, do you get the drift
we need peace yall, — call it

not a piece of peace
not a one night stand, flash in the pants peace
we're talking more than cheese, please, — call it

and more hospitals, schools, teachers, books,
theaters, museums, parks, ban the nukes
butter doesn't cut it

honey doesn't make it sweet
powdered milk doesn't keep it neat
we need peace yall, — call it

not a private room, no cameras allowed
wave and bow peace, — call it
more than a dialogue between east and west

we're talking world here
at best, some buildings may be left
we need peace yall, — call it

we need a people recognized peace, — call it
a people organized, galvanized, solarized, socialized,
computerized, glorified, sanctified,
dignified, never again horrified, dare you to
touch it peace, — call it

stand on line for that jack
no piecemeal peace
no erector set, silly puddy

humpty dumpty, funny duddy
leave the stars out of it peace, — call it
the stars are in it

as well as the sun and the moon
a heavy duty tune, — call it
a hundred million dollars to the contras

a hundred million dollars from social security
a hundred million dollars from healthcare
a hundred million dollars from daycare

a hundred million dollars from, who cares
peace, you better — call it
farmers losing their land, two farms a day

bombs are needed more than wheat or hay
peace, you better — call it
in vietnam the average american fighting age

was nineteen, a real live american dream
peace, you better — call it
in nicaragua fifty percent of the population

is fifteen years old, dance hall babies
digging trenches for the cold war
peace, you better — call it

who did grenada aggress
who and what did maurice bishop test
the u.s.?, please, peace, you better — call it

in south africa black children
are tortured and detained by lovers
of bombs and gold, not brains

peace, you better call it
the future could be a blast
ask eleanor bumpers, fred hampton,
edmond perry, emit till,
clifford glover, michael stewart,
michael griffith, randi evans,
yusef hawkins, claude reese

ask the police
or the millions gassed
peace, you better — call it

scoop of the day
the tension mounts
everyone counts

the native american's drums
warned us a long time ago
we were too slow

peace, the winners of lotto will burn as fast as the losers
peace, bill cosby is not enough
peace, the empire will not be around to strike back
peace, in the end, the color won't be purple
no matter who directs it
peace, you'll go whether you're wearing sneakers or
loafers, briefcase or backpack
peace, we've gone to the mountaintop several times
peace, we've seen jack and jill tumble down several hills
you better — call it

a hiroshima cloud grows in the persian gulf
a hiroshima cloud grows in howard beach
a hiroshima cloud grows in bensonhurst

a hiroshima cloud grows in greensborough
south carolina
a hiroshima cloud grows in the love canal

say what, is that cheese stopping you up?
you better — call it
nagasaki is a bombed birmingham church
nagasaki is an over crowded, rat infested welfare hotel
nagasaki is a crazed gunslinging man on a subway
you better — call it

call it
call it
call it

cherynoble was a belch compared to what
peace
karen silkwood's bones are still ticking
peace
three mile island is endless
peace

the pork eaters will fry
the vegetarians, buddhist, atheist, elitist,
winos, pornos — why? peace

even the mets
no matter the bet
eyeballs and flesh stuck on first base

nobody's safe
peace, c'mon, c'mon
a parade of tall ships is not peace

a stacking of chips, a maneuver of tanks,
war games with dummies and blanks
is not peace

do you want to glow
or do you want to grow, peace
pahpahpahpahpah, peace yall

you better call it, horde it, grab it, or stuff it
and sing the do / wop / drop / bye-bye song
oooooooooweeeeee
bye-bye

madness and a bit of hope

·

·

1
what is madness
is it an outbreak of dawn, a wild blood sun
killing this night
this touchless night

it is the wale of a full moon
over the breast of a homeless mother
or the shriek of stars
witnessing murder

to risk living
you encounter madness
broad based and picking its teeth
the insane sigh
and pull you to their chest

sometimes, you must stop breathing
to leave them
and leaving the insane
is again, madness

a run towards orchids
blooming in a field of broken glass
a terrain too dangerous to walk over
and running doesn't avoid the danger

but then, this is
the risk of living
the blood letting among flowers

2.
what is madness
a cacophony of voices
in our armpits
hurling us into stillness
banging our heads with memory

i remember when small
the voices were crystals
easy to hold and pray to
at night they were bells
listening to the wind in my breath

when small
the voices taught me how
to ride my bike down steep hills
how to turn sharp corners

the voices made me
laugh at the dark
and the darkened places
kept the voices hidden

from pointing fingers
of mommy
she — wanted to know
who i was talking with
she wanted to know

why i sang even when
daddy was drunk
beyond a reason
for being here

she wanted to know
what allowed me to sleep
in the middle of her crying
and why i never awoke with tears of my own

the voices
i never told mommy about the voices
and how they whispered me
into dancing to the edge of everything

how they hummed
as i curtsied for the old ladies
and kissed the sunken cheeks
of old men

how at times they riddled me
to a windowsill, or a bridge
or a razor, or daddy's whiskey
but just for fun

just to see me dance to
and away from another edge
the voices are such testers
when small, i never thought of failing

3.
now, tapping
behind my ears
awakening too many pieces
the voices are rivalry

jarring, rampant
between my fingers
between my toes
i hear them

even as i run towards the orchids
i hear them
belittling my escape

4.
what is madness
a seagull impaled on a fence
a cat walking into a river
a baby sucking needles in the center of a room
rain beating holes into the eyes of a dead dog

when did the voices
become
so diseased and angry
and whose strength do they use
to carry us to such unfamiliar places

they can pull triggers
they can throw us off rooftops
they can split us into uneven halves
whose strength do they use

6.
a man i know
is fighting these mutant voices
he is scraping them from his walls
dragging them from under his bed

somehow they have read
his books and his mind
they quote his fears
hear them, whose strength do they use

hear them, whose strength do they use

they are charging up this man's back with swords
an army paranoid of his every blink
they bulge his eyes
see them, whose strength do they use

the voices are taking this man's dark brown skin
and stretching it across his memory
he stands before himself like a crucifix
his palms showing the lines of too much and too many

a mother, two fathers, three brothers,
two sisters, two daughters, one son, two wives,
three college degrees, no job
i hear this man shouting at the voices

a cacophony of his own
a litany of statistics
of dark brown women and men
the number on ships

the number killed by whips
the number in chains, the number swung from ropes
the numbers, every number heavy in his throat
a malignant phlegm

i've seen this man try
and inch his skin away from the voices
seen him count the spots of light
left by other dark skins

and carry this number as if a
candle to his brain
illuminating the horrors
and when he speaks

it is of the women and men
ripped open in front of their mothers
it is of the fathers crippled by
the weight of silence

this man's tongue is thick
with the silence of dark brown fathers
and the voices dare him to speak
dare him to dare

these voices jealous
of this man's 46 unbending years
threaten him with death at any corner
threaten him with the lethal stare of a stranger

7.
what is madness
hot tar cooling on dark brown skin
pickled genitals in a jar

and when we run from these voices
we wish for the wings of eagles, for the grasp of hawks
a caravan of warriors in our sweat
our eyes screaming madness be still

not another dark brown body
will it take, not another
will it take to its rage ridden room
not another foot, tooth, or strand

of tightly coiled hair
this man and i poised against our walls
ready for attack
see us, our skin, our only weapon

8.
what is madness
the smell of orchids stronger than the smell of blood
how many pieces of glass embedded in my feet
i mustn't stop to look

no, i mustn't stop to look
i want these flowers
i want this sweet touch
risking life for beauty

risking sanity for love
a bit of hope covering my wounds
a bit of hope covering my wounds

a bit of

.

.

for us muscle women, when the bench press
gets depressing

.

.

we muscle women
do not only lift weights
we lift bottom

pull up the root
pop the nerve of it
and them

strip bottom raw and sour
snap guts like some
snap beans

stink from the slaughter
until nobody wants us
except ourselves

thank god

hints #13

.

.

the feet
are there
for the
taking

each toe
should be
embraced
the ankles

should
also be
involved
and don't

forget
to give
the arch
a little taste

hints # 6

.

.

it has
steeped
this black
coffee

take a sip
careful
it may burn
have a bite

of this fresh
jelly roll
chew slowly
this sweetness

earned

hints # 3

.

.

the meat
has been
well primed

but the
sauce must
thaw

a slow
heat
and

stir

hints # 4

·

·

if it is tired
let it sleep
let it curl
in its hairy nest

let it snore

and in the morning
as it gathers
under its tent
as it stretches

opening its one eye

i'll bring it
jam
i'll bring it
moon cakes

hints # 9

.

.

begin
at
lower
lip

proceed
to
chin
neck

clavicle loops
on to solar plexus
divide
bring breast across
in a handful

breathe
heavily along the ribs
scat down to the
naval basin

drop into bone
rock over pelvis
lay claim
in the thighs

and
then
just
hum

goodhousekeeping #18 (order)

.

.

rebecca is very organized
about her sex thing, it's number 17 on her daily agenda
except on sundays, when preparing and getting her
family off to church occupy spots 1-13
praise rebecca

which means the sweeping of floors
is knocked down to number 14
which makes bed making 15,
and toilet bowl scrubbing 16,
which means rebecca hangs up clothes at 17,
cleans strands of hair out of sinks at 18,
washes the breakfast dishes at the drop of 19,
and she then starts the big sunday meal at 20

which really annoys rebecca because of all the dishes
it puts on her for 21 and then her two itty-bitty ones
must bathe on 22 and 23, bathroom clean up is 24,
such a storm after the itty-bitty ones,
most times clean up is into 25
and then there's their favorite bedtime story for 26

and the glasses of water, oh the itty ones and their water
are 27 and 28, and the trips
to make wee wee are 29 and 30
rebecca taking a piss her damn self
(praise rebecca) is a sure fire 31,
and maybe she'll sit to drip for 32 and 33,
which has a great tendency to give her the push

she needs to take off her good church going clothes 34,
and splash some water on her face, 35,
rub some on her usual number 17, well hell, 36,
and soon she'll know she'll just run over to her husband
for a nice wet one 37,
he's been so busy with the sunday paper
a lot happening in the world,
probably even more since rebecca completed number 20
sundays are real hard on rebecca

praise rebecca

goodhousekeeping #13
(the well pampered kitchen)

.

.

she wanted a pretty kitchen
yes she did, she wanted a real live pretty kitchen
she really, really did, wanted it unlike her
mama's and unlike her granmas and unlike her
neighbor's down the hall

so, she painted her kitchen walls sun-rise orange
and she painted her kitchen cabinets sun-set orange
and she shopped in this store and that store,
trying to find the right shade of burnt orange
table and chairs
and curtains and linoleum

and she begged and cried to her landlord
for the closest thing to twilight orange
that he could find for a refrigerator and stove
she threatened to withold her rent if he didn't comply,
said if he did, she'd consider letting him see
the frog shaped mole on her left thigh

oh she wanted a pretty kitchen
a real live pretty, pretty kitchen and she looked in
a magazine and saw rose-pink tulip tiles and she worked
double time on her department store job

and she worked time and a half
at her telephone company job and she bought
them rose-pink tulip tiles
and she put some on the wall behind
her burnt orange stove

and she put some around the wall of
her painted burnt orange sink
and she put some on the sunset orange cabinets
for highlight she said,
just like a picture from one of them
home decor magazines she said,
'cause she wanted a pretty kitchen,
a real live pretty kitchen, sure to amaze and dazzle
and set the heart to skipping
pretty kitchen, unlike her mama's and her granma's
and her neighbor with the five kids down the hall

and she worked triple on her department store job
and she worked triple on her telephone company job
and she bought new pots with copper orange bottoms
and she hung them lavishly from a pegboard
and she bought sunrise orange cups
and swung them elegantly from fluorescent orange hooks
and she bought sun-set orange plates and
stacked them according to size and frequency of use
in her sunset orange cabinets

such a grand sight,
and not a drip from the faucet was allowed,
not a dish rag hanging out to dry was allowed,
not a roach, or a rat, or a man, or a child,
just like a commercial for spic and span,
ajax, or top job, she had a top job of a kitchen,
a real live pretty, hurt your eyes kitchen,
unlike her mama's
or her granma's or her neighbor
who had five kids and lived down the hall

and when asked the secret of her kitchen's beauty
meaning, does she clean it every day, reclean it every night
meaning, does she have a strong arm crew of women
come in on weekends with a mammoth supply
of brillo and bugspray and ammonia
meaning, does she pray, do magic tricks

she smiles as she stands at the door of her pretty kitchen
as if she's at the gates of some heaven and she says —
— it's simple and without a doubt,
i don't use the damn thing,
i just like standing here, checking it out

goodhousekeeping #17
(kitchen fable)

    .

    .

it was early in the morning
before sun or her children rose
and she was at the kitchen sink squeezing
pink liquid soap over the previous nights dishes
and she had pink curlers in her hair
and a pink, frayed, terrycloth robe drooped over her
shoulders
and a worn bra and an over bleached
pair of panties peeked
from under the pink robe every now and then

and she ran hot water over the dishes and over her hands
and she looked into a bubble and popped it with her spit
and then it happened
right there in the early morning, in her kitchen sink,
before her own never enough sleep eyes
rose mr. clean

with his gold earring in his left ear
and his big hands on his hips and his hips,
hands, face, legs all golden yellowish
with a pale green glow all around
and she put her soapy hands over her wide opened
mouth. then to her stiffened in disbelief neck
and mr. clean with his gold earring in his left ear,
and his hands on his hips,
and his hips all golden and muscular, winked at her
and sparks of light flew from his eyelid

and she covered her breast and mr. clean smiled and
sparks of light shot from his snow white teeth
and she picked up a nearby knife
and mr. clean said — i can make your work disappear —
and she held her robe closed with one hand
and raised the knife higher with the other
and mr. clean pulled on his gold earring
and the knife and every dirty dish disappeared

and she reached for her curlers
as though expecting them to go too
and mr. clean shook his gleaming, hairless head at the
stove and every pot and pan disappeared
and the stove sparkled
she swayed into a faint, her head bowed, her knees bent,
her eyes rolled, her hands flew way above her head
and mr. clean saw her go down and scooped her up
and held her close
& his ammonia and pine like sudsy smell revived her
and he said,
— i could make your life more enjoyable —

and he pulled on his gold earring in his left ear
and her curlers left, her robe went, and the worn bra
and over bleached panties were zapped away
and she was butt naked in the arms of mr. clean
she didn't know what to do, she was speechless
swore her eyes had gone totally bad

and mr. clean said —i could make it real good for you —
and he smiled and sparks of light covered her thighs
and in all her years of standing at her kitchen sink,
her thighs had never been touched by anything,
let alone light and she looked at her thighs all aglow,
she looked at her sink and stove all aglow
and she looked at a roach who had been watching
the whole damn thing
and she felt something warm
and itchy rise from her stomach to the tip of her head

and in all her years of being in the kitchen, she had never
been as warm before, and she had never been
held as close before
and she braved a look into mr. clean's golden eyes,
braved a touch of his gold earring
and somehow, from somewhere
words swelled in her neck and she said,
as she held on to the gold earring

—could you make me shine mister, could you really,
really, make me shine forever more —

"just say no"
or "ding dong the witch is dead, oh, the wicked old witch
is surely dead. yo ho!"

.

.

hurry, hurry
listen up
hear what
i have to say

i have the
real live
hookus pookus
juju words
make all the buggas and
funky ills fall
out the way

come on now
gather close
put whatever you're
doing down

because what i'm
talking about is magic
enough to give you power
make you world renowned

you can use it
if you're black
use it if you're
yellow, red, beige or white

use it if you're
one of those who is
afraid of being bumped
off in the night

women have fun saying it
dressing in their fineness
whenever it's time

men love whispering it
to themselves, it keeps
them firm, and pumping
in their prime

kids can learn it
right along with the
golden rules, it's
as basic as the
three Rs

and it's better than
those fairy tales, tooth
goddesses, santa claus or
wishing on silly old stars

now that i
have you listening
the spell has nearly
taken full hold of you

so put your
hands on your hips
make sure you're disgusted
thoroughly about something
and don't know what to think or do

then, open your mouth wide
fill your head with heaps of air

cross your eyes
until everything
disappears

then, exhale
as if it's your
last breath

and let these
words come forth
nice and slow
is best

"just say no"
those are the words
as easy as can be

"just say no"
those three words
will have you flying
high and free

from poor housing
        poor health
        poor schools
        poor love

"just say no"
over and over
there is no greater power
below or above

and i bet
in south africa
as soon as someone
sneaks Nelson and his men the words

he'll wrap "just say no"
around his tongue
and Botha and his boys
will do the bird

and what if
in hiroshima
as america dropped
the napalm

if the japanese
knew about "just say no"
everything would've
stayed so calm

for this is
new age power
not costing you zip
just let "just say no"
roll from the fullest
part of your bottom lip

and so what
if the federal budget
gives more money
to armies than
to people

those three words
are all we need
they will make us proud
make us equal

and if for
any reason
it feels as if
change for the good
is taking much to long

just string enough
of "just say nos"
together until you have
a pleasant,little song

hum it on
the unemployment line
hum it on a stalled,
overcrowded train

hum it while hungry
and sleeping in the rain

and if you're female
being battered for
not doing what you
were told

just stick out
your chest like a man
and sing those "just say nos"
loud, lady, sing them bold

i swear, it's
a wonder how we've become
blessed with such a light

i suppose the appropriate
thing to do is bow
our heads and thank
Nancy Reagan for all her
anti-drug fights

and yes, dear americans
the governments truly
on the people's side

the administration will
give all the banners, leaflets and pins
you need to decorate your community
in "just say no" pride

so, whenever
you're feeling
as though the world
should come to a hard,
screeching halt

go stand next to
your "just say no" sign
and in lightning speed
you'll have a world
with no faults

hope

.

.

flowers

.

.

in new york city
there are people

skin sun browned
hands earth worn

tongues as foreign
as their eyes

they push carts
filled with flowers

long stemmed, paper wrapped
and rubber banded too tightly

like the rest of the city
fragrance and color near gone

yet the people
push the flower carts

block after unyielding block
stopping to sell what they can

stopping to pray over
what they cannot

summer '89 at the art colony, again, the only black

.

.

more than a century
great, great grans
stood at an opened door

for some their skin
feeling too dark and
heavy to move too quickly

yet, they did move
gathered belongings
private parts

which had been cut away
preserved in jars
lovers still hanging from trees

names of parents
hidden in bones
names of unborn

hidden in sweat
they gathered these
at the opened door

they smelled of blood
freedom had whipped them before
how would they know

it wouldn't whip them again
how would they know
but, they walked through

sometimes, one by one
through the opened door
sometimes

one
by
one

m.l. king day, nyc, 1989

.

.

we are here
at one of the campsites
of the dream

still far from
the mountaintop
still

we the women
we the children
we the men

black, brown, red
yellow, white
we've heard the speeches

and prayers
we've been in the wars
we carry our dead

at times as casually
as air
the hopeful

and the wounded
sit closest
to the fire

soon it will
be morning
again

soon it will be
time to march
again

strength #11 (heroines)

.

.

what about
full moons and sojourner

slow music
and harriet

what about those
nights in the heat

when they didn't
have to run or hide

or pray
no speech or plea

to convince anyone
of their power

those nights
when they laid there

naked, alone or with another
clean sheets, one small candle

flowers in a glass
the slow easy rise

of their stomachs
the slow, easy spread

of their breast

bertha . . . ah, vencera
(dedicated to bertha calderon and the freedom loving
people of nicaragua)

•

•

in nicaragua
when my mother had become too weak for war

and could no longer stand and churn an empty pot
or brush the ashes from the baby's face

i thought one thing
bertha, ah vencera

bertha would stand my mother up
bertha would blow the ashes far away

bertha would find some corn for the pot
in nicaragua

whenever i saw my mother sitting on a road
with the blood of her son flooding her skirt

and his hard bones crushing her womaness
ah dios, i thought quickly

one thing, bertha, ah, vencera
bertha would wash my mother's skirt

ah, vencera
bertha would lift the weight from her womaness

in nicaragua
when without sleep, i heard my mother screaming

like a thousand wolves to the night
trying to pull dead dreams from her hair and eyes

trying to spit somoza's bitters from her mouth
mi madre

mi madre
one thing, bertha, ah vencera

bertha would sit with my mother
ah vencera, bertha would comb my mother's hair

cradle my mother beyond those screams
oh si, ah, vencera

in nicaragua
when i saw my mother kneel at my father's grave

feet cracked, no shoes, no flowers
one thing

one thing
ah vencera, bertha

bertha's hands would rub my mother's feet,
bertha's hands would place flowers on my father's grave

[86]

si, ah, vencera
and in nicaragua

when before god and man and gun
i saw my mother laying in a river

with bullets eating her breast
in the name of sandino, aviles, turcios

amador, escobar, perez
in the name of mi madre

and her love, and her power
ah vencera

i swallowed hard my own life
and thought the single thing

bertha, ah, vencera
bertha would suck the bullets from my mother's breast

cover the holes with a kiss from her own lips, ah vencera
clothe my mother in sky colors, ah vencera

and send my mother home like a soldier, ah vencera
ah vencera, oh si

ah vencera

hip hop meets winnie mandela

.

.

check out winnie mandela's stare on the cover of her book
her look be the book

word

her glare be chillin the air
word

she be threatenin, no sweatin
each mornin of the last twenty seven years
word

her look can cook
be her spear, be like this here no access wall between her
and the gun
word

no funnin, winnie's look be comin
put all those apartheid dogs on the run
word

and it always be like she got some of them
soweto kids under her lids
word

like when she blink, she always think
of how they took to the streets when the government said
they'd have to change up on their speech
word

you can see, winnie ain't about copin a plea
eyes be like angry hands throwin stones
word

bustin heads and hearts, winnie's stare be bone
word

can be like some fierce hurricane, twistin, turnin up
everythin, nothin be the same
word

be like bird through prison bars
word

this ain't drippin or trippin
winnie's gleam be like star
word

be like when her ole man nelson
finally got his arms 'round her waist
word

prison guards couldn't stand the sight
but it held them tight
a sweet taste
word

and then again, you see, winnie be
just a rockin in the rain
word

she be there tryin to gather up some music
to help gather up the pain
word

but she know she gonna be free
anybody lookin at her, yo, that's the first thing they see
word

and when alone at night,
i bet she lay her stare dead on that dark
the sure you're right winnie mandela mark
word

and she say with them eyes, she won't be denied
she got the might
word

so, easy, everything gonna be alright
word

now, that's what i'm talkin about
word

double dare '88

.

.

so here you are america
with a black man in your race
running towards your big white house
as if he owned the place

and the backstairs are not where he's heading
even though you keep showing him
those delivery boy signs
his beam is on your insidious front gate
and you, offended, swear to your glory that he's lost his
mind

you fan yourself with clippings of all the major poles
how could some chicken fed, black southern,
country boy dare to be so bold
why isn't he just satisfied with the whatever he already has

why, in the good ole days of america
his kind were cut and hung
for merely looking beyond their class
and then, i guess america, you're worried,
and rightfully so it seems
about all those other black children

who may start having presidential dreams
and what about the poor and homeless,
you've condemned to your streets
what will be their thoughts as they watch this brazen
black man

dance in your governmental heat
they may begin to think that there's something for them
in this great american vote
they may get back to reading
they may get back to writing
they may even dare to hope

for harry

.

.

yo, harry, always know this
that inspite of the diagnosis

you know man, totally and thoroughly
inspite of all this aids whatnot and therefore

these limp exclamation marks
these here medical technocrats want to put on

the tail end of your life
i mean, go on man

put a layer of snot over every thread
of this here death paraphernalia

this here rubber glove, gauze mask, sterilized solution
you know, that hold your breath, wait for a cure solution

that the humpty dumpty doctors and friends
who grow pity like rapunzel grew hair

always want to great you with
show them cats the finger, flash 'em

past all the gas in their face
like that man, 'cause you know how it is

yoyos always giving death the headstart
pumping up the zombies for prime time

harry, run 'em off the road
inspite of the i.v. and your always irrational b.p.

you stayed pretty
walked out of that hospital and bought yourself

one of the baddest leather jackets on the market
soft, black classic, like you harry

looking good man, like nothing had hold of you
except life
yeah, like that harry

inspite of it all man, you looked good baby,
you looked good

like that

deliver

.

.

knees up, legs spread
opening of cervix
a volcanoes pit
everything sits on a minute

begin breathing
howl of hurricane
sigh of tornadoes
gasp of earthquakes

breathe mama
kotex, white gown,
bible, more than bible
breathe mama

c'mon sugar breathe
aroma of rainbows
everything sits on a minute
want some music

violins, pianos
drum rolls, growls
concentrate on shadows on walls
breathe

everything sits on a minute
lady love, don't worry about farting, fart
don't worry about your lipstick, breathe
mama, the edge is at your eyelids

you're ready to push
more than steamroller, tank, bulldozer
push
lights out, moon gone

push
winter hail storm
monsoon rains, locust attack, drought
relax, slow breaths

no pushing
fetal heartbeat steady at 110
ocean heartbeat steady at 110
moon and sun steady at 110

everything sits on a minute
more than pathological
wouldn't you say
more than doctor spock

contraction
centuries of women stomping in her belly
contraction peaking
centuries of women wishing to be drunk

breathe mama
alto sax in her naval
centuries of women ice skating on her blood
centuries of pelees on swollen nipples

contraction, double peak
mount kilamanjaro
hold on mama
centuries of boiling bottles, boiling rags

centuries of nightstalking, counting every head twice
three times if tired
centuries of armed women saying-
death, don't touch my child

contraction end, ceasefire
pretty mama, your hair looks fine
open your legs mama
more than moses parting water

aisha has five, mona has ten
esther louise has twins
legs up sugar pie
c'mon girl

c'mon sweetheart
hold on
centuries of women grinding stars on her teeth
centuries of women peeing on sheets

centuries of women on all fours
mama, more than laser, radar, atomic,
nuclear, sonic
legs up

everything sits on a minute
push mama
part salmon swimming upstream
part bird flying south

part snake shedding skin
mama
part dinosaur, wolverine, witch
push

jackie died with her third
estelle left here without ever seeing her 13th
judy's in love with her oldest son
relax mama

more than soldier, deep sea diver, tight rope walker,
more than firefighter
more than houdini, goliath, noah
relax, breathe slowly

the world sits on a minute
contraction
hold on mama
centuries of women holding on

through government cutbacks, spend downs,
breathe mama
centuries of women breathing through
nuclear reactor melt downs, radiation fallout, toxic shock,

loneliness shock
breathing more than air
felicia has been trying for five years to have just one
a total eclipse, a meeting of planets

a spinning of an electron
breathe mama
don't worry about exposure
breathe

einstein had a theory for a bomb
columbus had boats
lincoln had proclamations
speilberg had a close encounter

breathe mama
power
more than diesel, hydraulic, supernatural
rod sterling could not imagine this

contraction
lou ellen changes paul's diapers with her mouth
hold on mama
umbilical upon umbilical

bear down mama
more than an fbi, cia crack down
push
ponce de leon looked for this

galileo looked for this
fred astaire, gene kelly, sandman sims, sammy davis
tried to dance this
sam cooke, otis redding, the beatles

tried to sing this
hitler tried to stop this
slavery tried to stop this
nuclear war will stop this

push mama
bombs bursting in air
francis scott key should have been watching this
push

populations
push
the invention of the wheel
right here mama

easy girl
you don't want to tear anything
push
why christ had to fight

why the africans had to fight
why the chinese had to fight
why the indians had to fight
why the jews had to fight

all right here mama
you've placed the world on a minute
head crowns
more than king or queen

more than president
or board of trustees
doing fine mama
eyes, nose, mouth

chin, neck
ease it mama
mozart, miles, bach, coltrane,
lillian hellman, betty carter,

virginia woolf, fannie lou hamer
doing fine
an arm, two arms,
ten fingers

margaret walker, james allen mcpherson
ease it
don't tear anything
more than flesh, bone,

more than black, white, yellow, beige
more than boy, girl,
tall, short
emil zola, che, wilma rudolph, tillie olsen,

alice childress
you can sigh a dust song
mama
two legs, ten toes

charlie parker, nina simone
naimah lateefah holmes
complete mama
complete

see, look at those eyes mama
look, at those eyes

for ben, and all the hued women and men

.

.

they hung a black poet in south africa
october 19th, 1985
his name was ben
the rope looped and swung
in a land where hued men are forced to bend

and i can tell
by the way my heart
and eyes swelled
that i was remembering what that rope had done
in alabama

in georgia, in the carolinas
of america where hued women and men
were forced to roll over and bend
and in south africa
october 19th, 1985

ben stood under the sun
a whistling, stone skipping, fish catching,
river wishing, wood carving, long walking man
stood roped and knotted under the sun
same sun

over hued men of mississippi, of texas,
of Louisiana, some big trees,
some small mind towns of america
ropes stung
ropes swung

and in south africa
a young black man loving family and land
never questioning his right to every drop
of water, every grain of sand
was knotted under the sun

glorious sun
that had pulled sweat, spit, bowels
from young hued women and men
who had fought wars for america
planted the peaches, the pecans

scared boll-weevil from the cotton
crows from the corn
danced the birth of america
yet were forced to sit without worth
never blowing the plentiful horn

you see, it wasn't that long ago
a hundred years or less
the rope was at its best
in america
and again, in south africa

october 19th, 1985, 8 am
ben was stripped from his waist to his neck
son of a black woman, lover of a black woman
father of a would have been, doctor, lawyer,
astronaut, magician, teacher, soldier,

musician, painter, stargazer, hellraiser
was stripped from his brave waist
to his hold it steady, ever ready neck
and remember, here, america
silhouettes of grinning faces

gathered like wolves
in all those hating places
where bodies black and wishing to
move about as free as the sea
were looped, and condemned to a tree

where white only signs
were strung like precious jewels
under the sun
which, very often were also the business tools
of america under the gun

as in south africa
ben's chin, from a family of 30 million
and more, was stiff and centered
over the knot, that looped over his chest
where bird poems nested

growing fat and wide
each time he swallowed
each time he opened his eyes
and remember, the chest of hued women and men
in america

pounding against american nights
heaving and praying against american days
which didn't allow them to walk the roads,
or shop the shops, or ride the trains,
or use the churches, or use the parks

or use their brains
just run the plow
and better not go insane
just run the plow,for a little
left over grain

and in south africa
october 19th, 1985
a land where colorless men kill to survive
a black man's chin, one of 30 million
and ever, ever more

was stiffly centered over the knot
over his chest, over his mother's eyes
that were told to stay away
threatened with jail if she dared to say goodbye
as they stripped and knotted her son

under the sun
as they spit on her womb's inalienable right
as they defecated in the memory
of her glorious swelling
some colorless men, who have stolen the land and laws

of south africa, yet kill to survive
hung a man and were very proud in the telling
and imagine, how black mothers of florida, mississippi
must have clenched their fist, gritted their teeth
when they were told that

how black mothers of virginia, dallas, kentucky
must have pounded the earth, swearing to give birth
again and again, when they were told that
how black mothers of new orleans must have cursed,
spat upon every tree

and the children
how would they be, hearing of papa being strung
would they grow up
blaming the sun
as ropes looped and knots stung

as they did in south africa 1985
to ben, a child of hued women and men
who refused to run
and i can name some in america
dick cooper, anthony grant, siles johnson,

zachariah walker
sometimes bunches in rows in america
strange fruit, seeded by sons of guns
who hooded and caped america
trying to smother the soul of america

burn the democratic goal
of america
and in south africa
ben, who dared to claim heart and stake
dared to challenge with pen and bare hands

the multi-headed dragon of hate
whose claws ripped through sharpsville
whose fires killed the corn of dimbaza
dared to challenge the lawless fate
of all those nights his father and mother

were forced to lay apart,
pray, dream and scheme apart
dared to imagine the days when the ever growing
30 million would vote, and hope
over all the land, no matter the language,

name, religion, or economic stand
and ben, brother of bheki, andries, sipho,
mohammed, many more
was aware, that because of his inability to be scared
that those banning against his hue

would try with money, guns and lies
to chill his power, like biko, still his eyes
and so, not far from today america
hued women and men daring their pores to
suck the tar and feathers, the hot oil

of america
daring their eyes
to blink or cry
when pieces of them were plucked and pickled in jars

as decoration for some of the drinking bars
in america
you see, there were would have beens
and could have beens
piled among the leaves of america

like ben, hued women and men
who could've written poems or songs
righting the wrongs
of america
as ben

in south africa, son of the charging
30 million and more
had talked to governments and gods
to change things
to mothers, lovers, moon, star

to hurry and rearrange things
under the sun
incredible sun
but the ears of the fearful, colorless few
disregards voices which challenges

their views
disregards anything which suggest or agrees
all people have the human right to be free
and when this freedom is never given
one to one

it may have to be taken
through the barrel of a gun
reluctantly, unfortunately
under the innocent sun
and i imagine as i swallow my screams, hold in my eyes

how ben
as many hued women and men
braced himself with that fact
how like thunder it made his body shout
even as his breath went under

that neither money, bullets,
or ropes which sting
can keep him from the peace fighting for truth brings

can keep his poems
from the hope they sing
so, ben, in the company of millions
of hued women and men
decided without narrowing

his mind or pride
that dying for truth
would be his life's prize
and as for ben, and all the other
hued women and men

ever hung, shot, beaten
burned, raped to bend
can't be far
but here, among us,
the remaining 30 million, and millions more

putting the fight and love
in our hearts and hands for the poor,
overworked, overtaxed, overhunted,
overmissed in whatever land
yes, here, fist and blood raised in a stronger stand

and knowing this
as screams rise
and strengths are put to the test
that such grand feelings may be doubted
may be drying among the leaves

but ben, and too many hued women and men
gave too much blood for us to disbelieve
and whenever necessary again and again
i'll hold my fears and see
the world rearranged

people of all hues whole and free
and know, like ben knew
that i and others of color and dissent
who want to stop the horror
however it is sent

are many, never few
and we will always be more
proud, powerful,
rich, poor

capable of joining for love
and joining for war
standing for freedom and peace above it all
never bending, no matter
how threatening, or tempting the call

and yes, more than yes
no matter the rise or fall
of what we do
being proud of our hues
and again, thanking ben

being proud of our women
being proud of our men

quilt

for granma patsy
equilla holmes, February 13, 1895-October 2, 1989

.

.

people write about lovers
wonders of river, bird, dirt, tree
people get involved with stars, moons,
mountains, their cats and dogs,
the bend of bridges, the curious motions of the sea

and lots go on about religion
infrequent sex, high finance,
designer clothes, hairdos, jewels,
foods, incessant t.v.
but, at the risk of sounding unhip

uninformed, backward, unread,
dull and whatever else the case may be
i want to say a bit about what
my granma's quilt
stirs up in me

diamond shaped pieces
of the niger and nile
ripples of pyramids and sphinx
tiny squares of palmwine, cassava
laying in concentric circles

at my feet
octagons of kente clothe,
triangles of red satin, clusters of alpaca,
swirls of kuskus, loops of fufu,
fried chicken, cornbread,

bows of sweet potato pie
over me, when i sleep
rectangles of slaveships
striped strips of leg chains
knots of lead weights

hexagons of whipped backs
jagged gray pieces of genitals in jars
scarlet bands of raped women
when i sleep
pentagons of rope tied tight around a neck

appliques of houses burning
in a cruel white, southern heat
mississippi delta in green velvet
over me when i sleep

black woolly patches
of cotton picking, rough burlap edges
of ants stinging, one or two leather spots
of snakes biting, oceans of oval shaped
gospel singing

arches of linen magnolia, honeysuckle
and mahalia jackson
over me, when i sleep
maroon felt buttons of canned sugar beets,
overlays of creamy silk senior choir sundays

swatches of advice about no money mondays
tough double stitching around the magenta
wool of dred scott
tougher still around the mohair patch of little rock
back stitching for harriet, frederic, fannie lou, nat,
sojourner, biko, josina

reinforcement with an array of angora blues
for bessie, billie, ma rainie
i believe in the night they pour
their way down all over me
and i got

lena as a long, beige velvet patch,
parker, mountain of herringbone tweed,
nina streaming with red, violet crepe,
coltrane center spreading hot chocolate lace,
ella and sarah dashes of divine kelly green,

the duke cashmere moons woven in and out
of the whole darn place
harlem and soweto, big base stitches
running real close to my ear
got big maple brown, corduroy decagons

of malcolm, martin, fred, george, emit
stabilizing the rear
vietnam slip stitches at the corners,
world war three pulls at the seams,
sea green terrycloth circles for labor pains at the borders

rose red tassels of new births
dangling in between
lavender ribbons of children
spinning with the dukes cashmere moons

walnut and cinnamon brown polka dot
beep boop women bouncing in the lining
from some sam cooke tune,
stuffing of dreambooks, bible, wedding pictures,
dried flowers, bat wings, bluejays,

fireflies, welfare checks, unpaid bills,
padded bras soaked with wonder
of them good ole backseat thrills
and those peppermint smells and coco,
cactus juice and yucca trees

ivory snowball fights, busrides, boatrides,
double dutch, dodgeball, rollercoaster, spooky house,
dandelion wishes blown all over me
for you see,
my granma, texas born, kansas raised

didn't have a car, big house, jewels,
fur coats, boats, a college course,
stereo, or a tv,
what she had was twelve brothers and sisters,
five children

and 94 years of history
and every birthday, special occasion
or just as a good deed
she'd cut and sew whatever she had seen and knew
and make a quilt for me

and no matter how dark or cold my house,
how unkempt or empty my bed,
whether or not the food's low,
roaches roaming free,
rent zooming way over my head

everyday, when i get tired
of fighting and smiling in the rough
i lay a while under them stars, moons, oceans
of blackfolks my granma gave me
and feel real free, sure enough

hints #35

·

·

what war
and nature
have not
taken

let us
bring
to bed
tuck in

tell a
happy
ending
story

leave on
a small
light

hello
.

.

and
between
these rocks

and
these
hard places

i'm,
making
diamonds